POPULAR SONGS
HAL LEONARD
STUDENT PIANO LIBRARY

Four Hands on Broadway

Eight Duets for One Piano, Four Hands

Arranged by Fred Kern

CONTENTS

ISBN 978-1-4950-2778-4

HAL•LEONARD®
CORPORATION
7777 W. BLUEMOUND RD. P.O. BOX 13819 MILWAUKEE, WI 53213

Visit Hal Leonard Online at
www.halleonard.com

And All That Jazz

from CHICAGO

Words by Fred Ebb
Music by John Kander
Arranged by Fred Kern

4

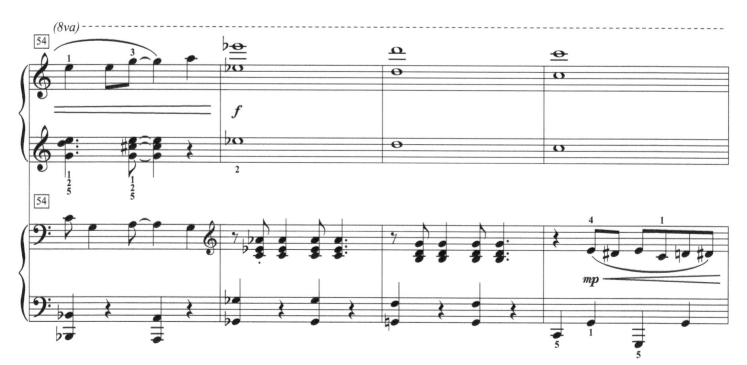

Anything You Can Do

from the Stage Production ANNIE GET YOUR GUN

Words and Music by
Irving Berlin
Arranged by Fred Kern

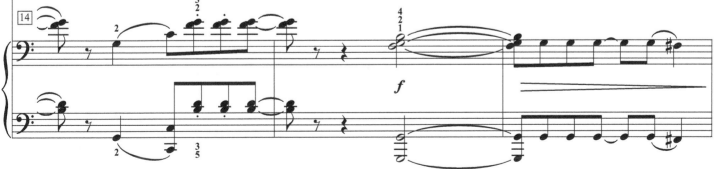

Do You Hear the People Sing?

from LES MISÉRABLES

Music by Claude-Michel Schönberg
Lyrics by Alain Boublil,
Jean-Marc Natel and Herbert Kretzmer
Arranged by Fred Kern

I Whistle a Happy Tune

from THE KING AND I

Lyrics by Oscar Hammerstein II
Music by Richard Rodgers
Arranged by Fred Kern

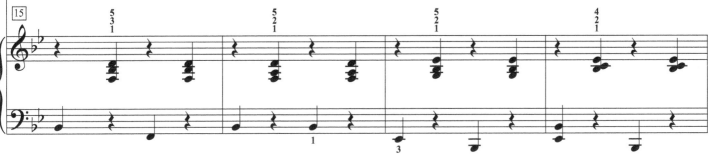

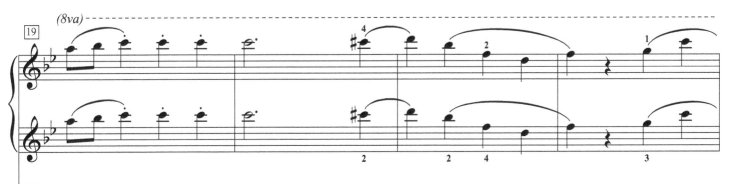

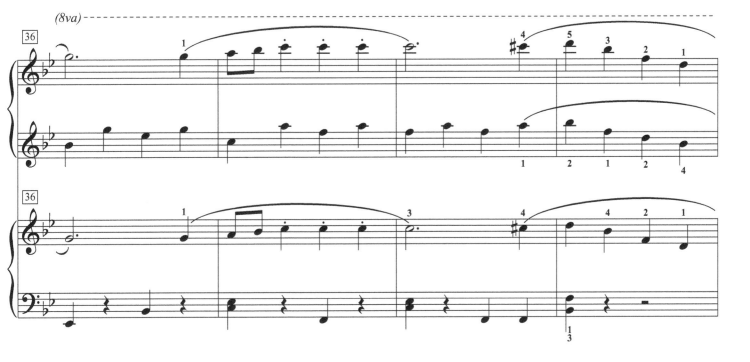

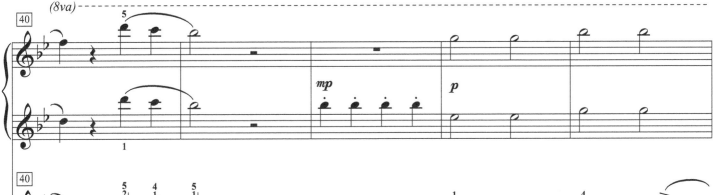

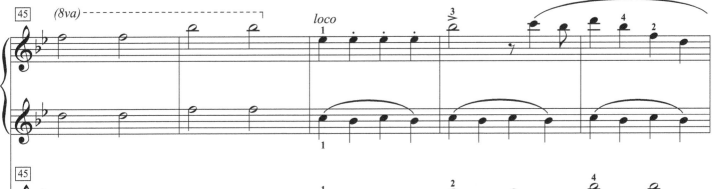

In My Own Little Corner

from CINDERELLA

Lyrics by Oscar Hammerstein II
Music by Richard Rodgers
Arranged by Fred Kern

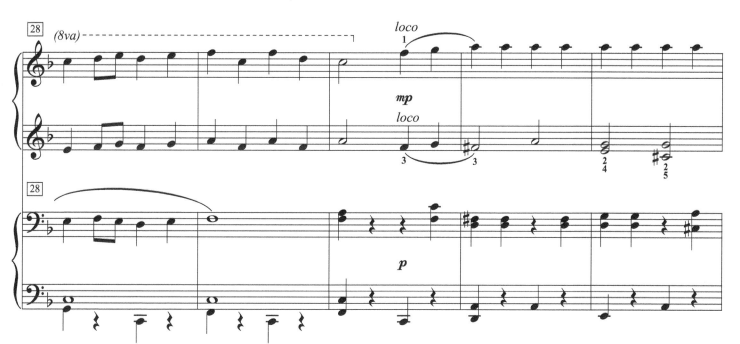

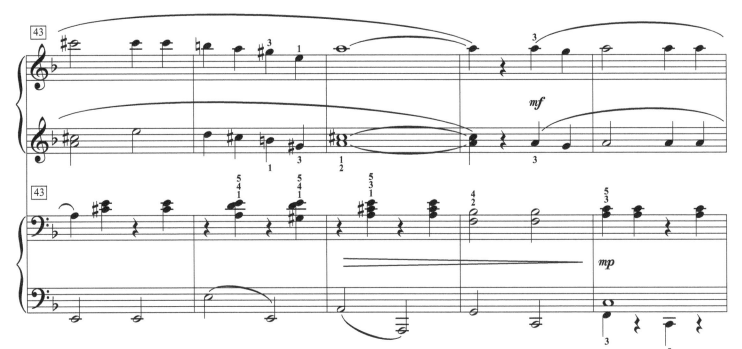

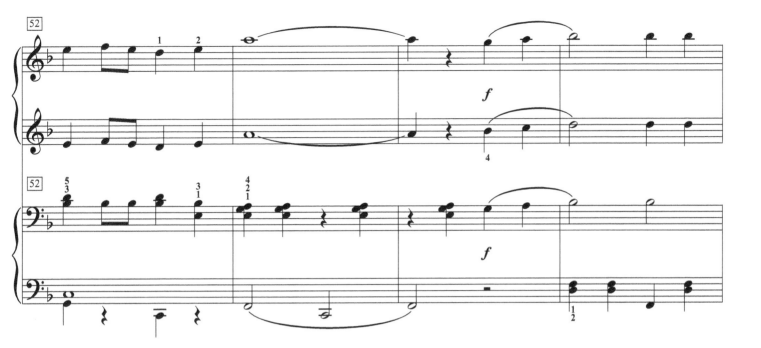

Put On a Happy Face

from BYE BYE BIRDIE

Lyric by Lee Adams
Music by Charles Strouse
Arranged by Fred Kern

31

It's the Hard-Knock Life/Easy Street

from the Musical Production ANNIE

Lyric by Martin Charnin
Music by Charles Strouse
Arranged by Fred Kern

"It's the Hard-Knock Life"
Moderately, with a tough edge (♩ = 120)

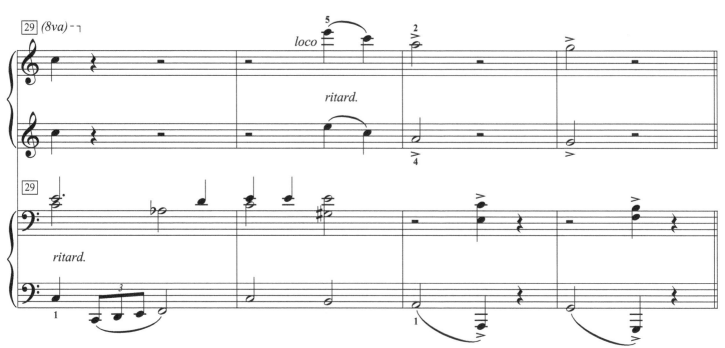

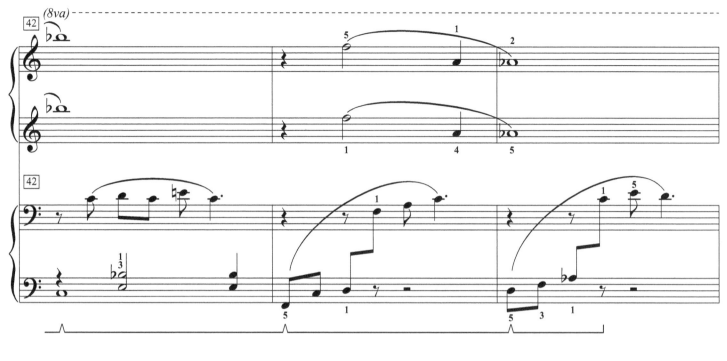

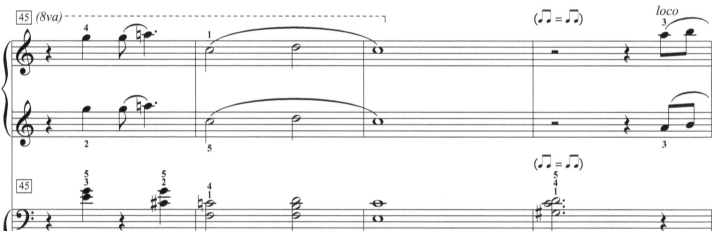

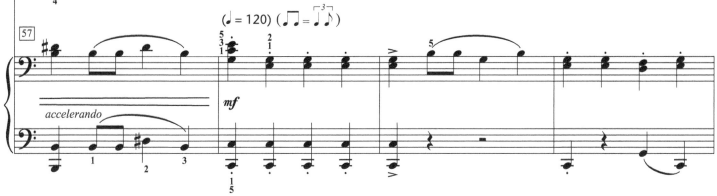

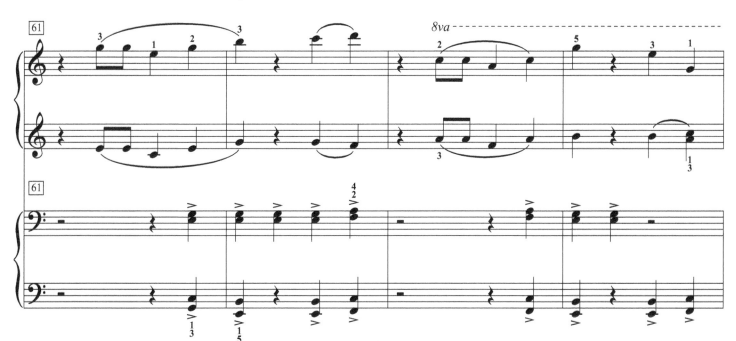

Seventy Six Trombones

from Meredith Willson's THE MUSIC MAN

By Meredith Willson
Arranged by Fred Kern

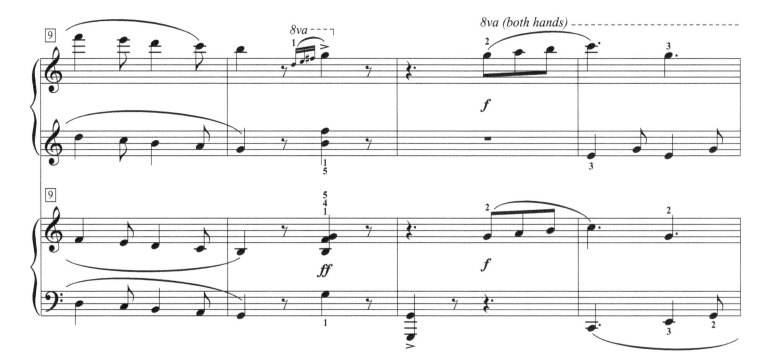

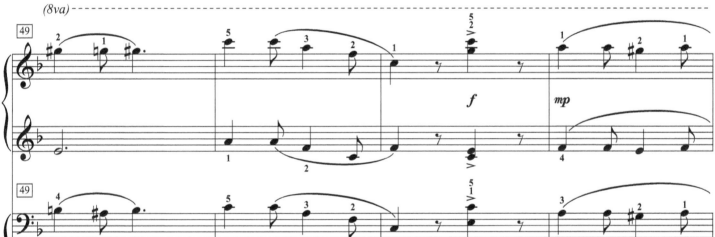

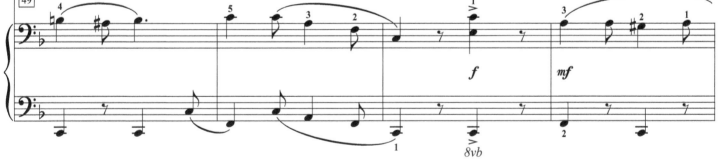

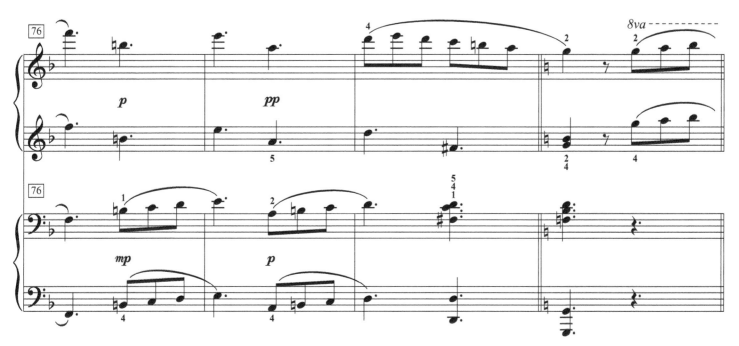

COMPOSER SHOWCASE
HAL LEONARD STUDENT PIANO LIBRARY

This series showcases great original piano music from our **Hal Leonard Student Piano Library** family of composers, including Bill Boyd, Phillip Keveren, Carol Klose, Jennifer Linn, Mona Rejino, Eugénie Rocherolle and more. Carefully graded for easy selection, each book contains gems that are certain to become tomorrow's classics!

BILL BOYD

JAZZ BITS (AND PIECES)
Early Intermediate Level
00290312 11 Solos.............................$7.99

JAZZ DELIGHTS
Intermediate Level
00240435 11 Solos.............................$7.99

JAZZ FEST
Intermediate Level
00240436 10 Solos.............................$7.99

JAZZ PRELIMS
Early Elementary Level
00290032 12 Solos.............................$6.99

JAZZ SKETCHES
Intermediate Level
00220001 8 Solos...............................$7.99

JAZZ STARTERS
Elementary Level
00290425 10 Solos.............................$7.99

JAZZ STARTERS II
Late Elementary Level
00290434 11 Solos.............................$7.99

JAZZ STARTERS III
Late Elementary Level
00290465 12 Solos.............................$7.99

THINK JAZZ!
Early Intermediate Level
00290417 Method Book.........................$10.99

TONY CARAMIA

JAZZ MOODS
Intermediate Level
00296728 8 Solos...............................$6.95

SUITE DREAMS
Intermediate Level
00296775 4 Solos...............................$6.99

SONDRA CLARK

FAVORITE CAROLS FOR TWO
Intermediate Level
00296530 5 Duets..............................$7.99

THREE ODD METERS
Intermediate Level
00296472 3 Duets..............................$6.95

MATTHEW EDWARDS

CONCERTO FOR YOUNG PIANISTS
FOR 2 PIANOS, FOUR HANDS
Intermediate Level Book/CD
00296356 3 Movements $16.95

CONCERTO NO. 2 IN G MAJOR
FOR 2 PIANOS, 4 HANDS
Intermediate Level Book/CD
00296670 3 Movements........................$16.95

PHILLIP KEVEREN

MOUSE ON A MIRROR
Late Elementary Level
00296361 5 Solos...............................$6.95

MUSICAL MOODS
Elementary/Late Elementary Level
00296714 7 Solos...............................$5.95

SHIFTY-EYED BLUES
Late Elementary Level
00296374 5 Solos...............................$6.99

TEX-MEX REX
Late Elementary Level
00296353 6 Solos...............................$6.99

CAROL KLOSE

THE BEST OF CAROL KLOSE
Early Intermediate to Late Intermediate Level
00146151 15 Solos.............................$12.99

CORAL REEF SUITE
Late Elementary Level
00296354 7 Solos...............................$6.99

DESERT SUITE
Intermediate Level
00296667 6 Solos...............................$7.99

FANCIFUL WALTZES
Early Intermediate Level
00296473 5 Solos...............................$7.95

GARDEN TREASURES
Late Intermediate Level
00296787 5 Solos...............................$7.99

ROMANTIC EXPRESSIONS
Intermediate/Late Intermediate Level
00296923 5 Solos...............................$8.99

WATERCOLOR MINIATURES
Early Intermediate Level
00296848 7 Solos...............................$7.99

JENNIFER LINN

AMERICAN IMPRESSIONS
Intermediate Level
00296471 6 Solos...............................$7.99

ANIMALS HAVE FEELINGS TOO
Early Elementary/Elementary Level
00147789 8 Solos...............................$7.99

CHRISTMAS IMPRESSIONS
Intermediate Level
00296706 8 Solos...............................$7.99

JUST PINK
Elementary Level
00296722 9 Solos...............................$7.99

LES PETITES IMAGES
Late Elementary Level
00296664 7 Solos...............................$7.99

LES PETITES IMPRESSIONS
Intermediate Level
00296355 6 Solos...............................$7.99

REFLECTIONS
Late Intermediate Level
00296843 5 Solos...............................$7.99

TALES OF MYSTERY
Intermediate Level
00296769 6 Solos...............................$8.99

MONA REJINO

CIRCUS SUITE
Late Elementary Level
00296665 5 Solos...............................$5.95

JUST FOR KIDS
Elementary Level
00296840 8 Solos...............................$7.99

MERRY CHRISTMAS MEDLEYS
Intermediate Level
00296799 5 Solos...............................$7.99

MINIATURES IN STYLE
Intermediate Level
00148088 6 Solos...............................$7.99

PORTRAITS IN STYLE
Early Intermediate Level
00296507 6 Solos...............................$7.99

For full descriptions and song lists, and to view a complete list of titles in this series, please visit www.halleonard.com

EUGÉNIE ROCHEROLLE

**ENCANTOS ESPAÑOLES
(SPANISH DELIGHTS)**
Intermediate Level
00125451 6 Solos...............................$7.99

JAMBALAYA
FOR 2 PIANOS, 8 HANDS
Intermediate Level
00296654 Piano Ensemble.....................$9.99

JAMBALAYA
FOR 2 PIANOS, 4 HANDS
Intermediate Level
00296725 Piano Duo (2 Pianos) $7.95

TOUR FOR TWO
Late Elementary Level
00296832 6 Duets..............................$7.99

TREASURES
Late Elementary/Early Intermediate Level
00296924 7 Solos...............................$8.99

CHRISTOS TSITSAROS

DANCES FROM AROUND THE WORLD
Early Intermediate Level
00296688 7 Solos...............................$6.95

LYRIC BALLADS
Intermediate/Late Intermediate Level
00102404 6 Solos...............................$8.99

POETIC MOMENTS
Intermediate Level
00296403 8 Solos...............................$8.99

SONATINA HUMORESQUE
Late Intermediate Level
00296772 3 Movements $6.99

SONGS WITHOUT WORDS
Intermediate Level
00296506 9 Solos...............................$7.95

THREE PRELUDES
Early Advanced Level
00130747 ....$8.99

THROUGHOUT THE YEAR
Late Elementary Level
00296723 12 Duets.............................$6.95

ADDITIONAL COLLECTIONS

ALASKA SKETCHES
by Lynda Lybeck-Robinson
Early Intermediate Level
00119637 8 Solos...............................$7.99

AMERICAN PORTRAITS
by Wendy Stevens
Intermediate Level
00296817 6 Solos...............................$7.99

AN AWESOME ADVENTURE
by Lynda Lybeck-Robinson
Late Elementary Level
00137563...$7.99

AT THE LAKE
by Elvina Pearce
Elementary/Late Elementary Level
00131642 10 Solos and Duets.................$7.99

COUNTY RAGTIME FESTIVAL
by Fred Kern
Intermediate Level
00296882 7 Rags...............................$7.99

MYTHS AND MONSTERS
by Jeremy Siskind
Late Elementary/Early Intermediate Level
00148148 9 Solos...............................$7.99

PLAY THE BLUES!
by Luann Carman (Method Book)
Early Intermediate Level
00296357 10 Solos.............................$9.99

HAL•LEONARD® CORPORATION
7777 W. BLUEMOUND RD. P.O. BOX 13819 MILWAUKEE, WI 53213